Supreme Court Justice

RUTH BADER GINSBURG

by Jack L. Roberts

Gateway Biography
The Millbrook Press
Brookfield, Connecticut

Library of Congress Cataloging-in-Publication Data
Roberts, Jack L.
Ruth Bader Ginsburg : Supreme Court Justice / by Jack L. Roberts.
p.   cm. — (Gateway biography)
Includes bibliographical references and index.
Summary: The life story of Ruth Bader Ginsburg, the
second woman to become a Supreme Court Justice in
U.S. history, emphasizing Ginsburg's work to end
discrimination against women under the law.
ISBN 1-56294-497-5 (lib. bdg.)   ISBN 1-56294-744-3 (pbk.)
1. Ginsburg, Ruth Bader—Juvenile literature.   2. Judges—United
States—Biography—Juvenile literature.   3. Sex discrimination
—Law and legislation—United States—History—Juvenile
literature. [1. Ginsburg, Ruth Bader.   2. Judges.   3. United
States.   Supreme Court—Biography.   4. Women—Biography.
5. Sex discrimination against women.]   I. Title.   II. Series.
KF8745.C56R63   1994   347.73'2634—dc20
[347.3073534]   93-39015   CIP   AC

Published by The Millbrook Press
2 Old New Milford Road
Brookfield, Connecticut 06804

Ruth Bader Ginsburg

*President Bill Clinton introduces his nominee for
the Supreme Court, Ruth Bader Ginsburg. He spoke
of how she had worked for many years for fairer
treatment of women and others under the law.*

At *exactly 11:33 P.M.* on Sunday, June 13, 1993, Ruth Bader Ginsburg received the most important telephone call of her life. The call was from the President of the United States, Bill Clinton. He was phoning from the White House kitchen to offer Ginsburg a job.

It wasn't just any job, though. It was a job as a justice (or judge) on the Supreme Court of the United States. The U.S. Supreme Court is the highest court in America. Only nine justices sit on the Court. Their job is to decide significant and difficult legal questions that often govern how we live.

The next day, President Clinton held a press conference in the Rose Garden at the White House. He wanted to introduce his nominee to the Supreme Court. If approved by the United States Senate, Ginsburg would become only the second woman in history to sit on the highest court in the nation.

In speaking about Ginsburg on that sunny afternoon, Clinton said that she was one of our nation's best judges. "Throughout her life," he told the press, "she has repeatedly stood for the individual, the person less well-off, the outsider in society, and has given those people greater hope by telling them they have a place in our legal system."

Then Ginsburg spoke. The small, trim grandmother of two, her hair pulled behind her head in a tight bun, walked to the microphone. She thanked the President for nominating her to this important job and promised to work hard to live up to his expectations. She also thanked the many people who had helped her throughout her career. Then she added a very personal comment.

"I have a last thank-you," she said. "It is to my mother, Celia Amster Bader, the bravest and strongest person I have known, who was taken from me much too soon. I pray that I may be all that she would have been had she lived in an age when women could aspire and achieve and daughters are cherished as much as sons."

Her comment brought tears to the President's eyes. He knew that Ginsburg, like many other women throughout America in the 1960s and 1970s, had often not had the same job opportunities as men. He also knew that her rise to the top of her field had been a long and difficult one — one that

Ginsburg speaking from the White House Rose Garden. She talked of fulfilling dreams as her mother could not have done because of unfair treatment of women.

Ruth during her high-school years. Although she was well liked, she didn't believe very strongly in her ability to excel.

In 1946, Ruth began her freshman year at James Madison High School in Brooklyn — a school that has produced dozens of famous or noted people in politics, medicine, education, and the entertainment field. For the next four years, Ruth (or Kiki, as she was often called) was an active and popular young girl. She played in the school band, worked on the school newspaper, and was treasurer of the "Go-Getters" Club, a student pep group.

But, according to one friend, Ruth wasn't very confident about her abilities. "She never thought she did well on tests," says the friend, "but, of course, she always aced them."

Ruth also kept a lot of things to herself. One of those things was the fact that her mother had cancer. In June 1950, on the day before Ruth was going to graduate from high school, her mother died at the age of forty-seven.

In the fall of 1950, Ruth left home for college at Cornell University in Ithaca, New York. There, she majored in government. She also joined a group called the Women's Self-Governance Association.

During her first year at Cornell, Ruth met her future husband, Martin Ginsburg, a year ahead of her at the university. For the next three years they dated, and by the time she was in her third year and he was about to graduate, everyone knew the relationship was serious.

Like many young college students, the couple often talked about what they wanted to do after they graduated. Neither one was sure, but Ruth thought she might be interested in studying law. "That a lawyer could do something that was personally satisfying and at the same time work to preserve the values that have made this country great," she later said, "was an exciting prospect for me."

Ruth and Martin did decide on one thing. They thought it would be a good idea if they both went into the same field. That way, they would always have something in common to talk about. Finally, they decided that Martin would apply to Harvard Law School in Cambridge, Massachusetts. He was accepted and began school there in 1953.

In June 1954, Ruth graduated from Cornell. That same month, she and Martin Ginsburg were married at the home of his parents. At about the same time, Martin went into the Army and the newlyweds moved to Fort Sill, Oklahoma, where he was stationed.

During this time, Ruth Ginsburg learned about discrimination against women firsthand. Soon after they moved, she got an office job at which she did extremely well. Then she got pregnant. As soon as her employer found out she was going to have a baby, he demoted her, which means he gave her a lower-level job than the one she had.

This must have troubled Ginsburg greatly. A man would not have been demoted in his job just because his wife was going to have a baby. Was it fair for a woman to be treated differently? Today, it is against the law to demote a woman in a job just because she is expecting a baby.

In 1955, Ginsburg gave birth to a baby daughter, whom she named Jane Carol. She also started thinking more seriously about going to law school — particularly to Harvard Law School, where her husband would be returning in the fall of 1956.

But there were at least three reasons why Gins-

The newlywed Ginsburgs. Shortly after they were married, the couple moved to Oklahoma. Martin entered the Army and Ruth entered the workplace, where she learned how unfairly women were often treated.

burg was not sure she should go to law school. First, she questioned whether she had "sufficient aptitude" for the law. Was she really smart enough to be successful in law school? It was a question she must have asked herself time and time again. Second, she discovered that few people, except for her husband, thought it was a good idea for her to go to law school. Even her own father thought it was more "sensible" for her to become a teacher. Finally, if she was going to go to law school, she wanted to go to Harvard. Yet, at that time, no woman had ever been admitted to Harvard Law School.

As she thought about what she wanted to do, she must have thought about how difficult it would be to take care of a little baby and her family and go to school at the same time. She must have also remembered how — only a few years earlier — she and her husband had talked about going into the same field.

Finally, she made up her mind. She applied to Harvard and was accepted. It was the first time Harvard Law School admitted women. Ginsburg was one of only nine women in a class of more than four hundred. So, that fall, both Martin and Ruth Ginsburg went to Cambridge, Massachusetts, to attend law school together.

Years later, Ginsburg said that she decided to become a lawyer because she felt she could do that job better than any other. "I have no talent in the arts," she once said, "but I do write fairly well." She also said she is able to think through problems very clearly.

In her first year of law school, Ginsburg learned how unwelcome women were in the field of law. The dean of the law school had invited the nine women students to his home for tea. Then, one by one, he spoke with each woman, asking her why she was there. "Do you realize," he asked Ginsburg sarcastically, "that you are simply taking the place of a qualified man?" It was a remark she would never forget.

In 1958, Ginsburg's husband graduated from Harvard Law School and got a job in New York City. So Ginsburg transferred to Columbia Law School, where she was one of only ten women. (Today, most law schools have almost as many women as men.)

At Harvard Law School, where this photo was taken, Ginsburg excelled. She served on the Harvard Law Review. Only the best students are selected to work on the Review, an important publication.

At Columbia Ginsburg earned the nickname "Ruthless Ruthie" for the way she attacked her schoolwork. As a result, the young woman who worried about whether she had the "aptitude" for law tied for first in her class when she graduated in 1959. But she would soon learn that even being first in your class didn't mean a great deal if you were a woman.

Imagine not being able to get a job you wanted simply because of your sex. In the 1960s there were many jobs that people thought only men should have. And there were other jobs that people said only women should have.

For example, in the 1960s men could not become flight attendants for major airlines. Those jobs were held only by women. At the same time, women could not become fire fighters or police officers. Those were considered to be jobs only for men.

When Ruth Bader Ginsburg graduated from law school, she wanted to become a law clerk for a justice of the U.S. Supreme Court. A law clerk helps the justice research cases and does other kinds of legal work.

In order to be considered for such work, a person must have two basic qualifications. First, he or she must graduate at the top of the class. Second, the student must graduate from a top law school. Ginsburg qualified on both counts. She had graduated from Columbia Law School — one of the best law schools in the country — and she had tied for first place in her class.

Yet, despite her outstanding qualifications, no one would hire her. The dean of Harvard Law School recommended her to Justice Felix Frankfurter of the U.S. Supreme Court. He turned her down flat, saying simply: "I don't hire women." He then smugly added: "Does she wear skirts? I can't stand girls in pants."

Even judges on lower courts refused to hire her, often with strange excuses. One judge, for example, said he couldn't hire her because he cursed too much. He said his foul language would make her too uncomfortable to be around him.

Ginsburg also tried to get a job with a major law firm. She must have sent out dozens of applications.

During the early 1960s, many people thought women should work only at jobs in which they served men, like the secretary shown here. Ruth Bader Ginsburg had trouble finding work as a lawyer because of such notions of a woman's "proper" place in the working world.

But only two even agreed to interview her. Neither offered her a job.

So she decided that maybe she would teach at a law school. But no law school at that time had a woman on its faculty. And none was ready to hire a woman, either.

There were a number of reasons why Ginsburg found it so difficult to get a job in the law field. One reason was that she was a woman. Another reason was that she was Jewish. Many of the top law firms in the country were only just beginning to hire Jews. And still another reason was that she was a mother. No one wanted to hire a woman with children. Employers were afraid that women who had children would not be able devote enough time to their work.

Any one of those reasons might have kept Ginsburg from getting a job she wanted. But all three together slammed the door shut on her opportunities. As Ginsburg later explained, "To be a woman, a Jew and mother to boot, that combination was a bit much."

Finally, Ginsburg did get a job — one that she was clearly overqualified for. It was a job as a legal secretary. It was one of the few jobs that many men at that time felt women could do. Even Chief Justice Warren Burger once said that women make the best secretaries because of their typing ability.

In her struggle to get a job, Ginsburg had learned firsthand about sex discrimination. She learned that women in the work force were not treated the same as men. And she must have vowed then and there to do something about it in the future.

In 1963, *Ginsburg* became one of the first women in the United States to get a job as a law professor. She became an assistant professor at Rutgers School of Law in New Brunswick, New Jersey. Two years later she became pregnant with her second child. By now, however, she knew enough about discrimination against women to know that she had to keep her pregnancy secret. She wore baggy clothes, so that no one could tell she was expecting a baby.

Ginsburg was beginning to think more about women's rights — or, more exactly, about women's lack of basic civil rights. She thought a lot about how women often did not have the same opportunities as men. And she thought about how society, in general, viewed women. Even the law school textbooks at that time often contained shocking statements about women. For example, one textbook on property law stated, ". . . land, like woman, was meant to be possessed."

By the late 1960s many women like Ginsburg were speaking out about women's rights. They were also organizing themselves to fight for fairer treatment.

Their struggle for equal rights, however, had begun more than one hundred years earlier. In 1848, Elizabeth Cady Stanton organized a group of women to fight for equal rights, particularly the right to vote. It took until 1920 for women to gain that right. After that, interest in women's rights seemed to lessen for a while.

Then, in 1966, a group called the National Organization for Women (NOW) was formed. The purpose of the group was to gain political, economic, and social equality with men, including equal pay for equal work.

As the 1960s progressed, American women came together for greater equality in the workplace and in many aspects of their lives. This photo shows women rallying for unity. Ruth Bader Ginsburg's commitment to women's rights also grew during the 1960s.

The issue of equal pay for equal work was one that Ginsburg understood very well. When she began teaching at Rutgers University, she discovered that women professors were paid less than men for doing the same job. She believed this was not only unfair, but that it should be illegal. So she went to the dean to complain. For Ginsburg it was just the beginning of her work involving sex discrimination.

While she taught at Rutgers, she also took on some cases for the American Civil Liberties Union (ACLU). Lawyers for the ACLU work on cases that involve basic rights of an individual. For example, one case involved a New Jersey law that said that teachers who got pregnant had to quit their teaching jobs. The law also said that those teachers did not have an automatic right to get their jobs back once the baby was born. Ginsburg thought this law was wrong, so she went to court to get it changed — and she won.

Ginsburg taught at Rutgers for nine years, where she was said to be an excellent teacher, even though, as one person explained, she was "a little dull." Then in 1972 she got a job as a full professor at Columbia Law School. She was the first woman to be hired by Columbia as a full professor. She was also the first woman to receive tenure. Tenure means that a professor cannot be fired from a job unless it can be proved that he or she is seriously lacking in the necessary skills for that job. Nineteen years later, at age thirty-eight, Ginsburg's daughter also became a tenured law professor at Columbia.

Ginsburg *never imagined* herself a pioneer. Yet during the 1970s that's exactly what she became — a pioneer for women's rights. During those years she argued six very important sex discrimination cases in front of the Supreme Court — the court of which she is now a member. Those cases had to do with laws or policies that treated men and women differently. She won five of them.

In one 1973 case, for example, she took on the U.S. military. The U.S. military gave health care and other benefits to the families of the men and women in the service. But it gave larger benefits to the wives of men in the service than it gave to the husbands of women in the service. Ginsburg said

Ginsburg in her law professor's robes at Columbia University, where she blazed many trails.

Martin Ginsburg with Ruth's Columbia picture on his desk. Both believed strongly in equal rights for men and women. "I have been supportive of my wife since the beginning of time and she has been supportive of me," he said.

this was wrong. So she took the case to the Supreme Court — and won. Today, spouses of servicemen and servicewomen get the same benefits.

Ginsburg wasn't interested only in women's rights. She was interested in equal rights for all people — both men and women. In 1976 an Oklahoma law said that women could buy alcoholic beverages if they were eighteen years old. Men, on the other hand, had to be twenty-one. Ginsburg felt that this law was not fair because it did not treat men and women equally. She took the case to the Supreme Court and won. The law was changed.

As a result of this important work in the 1970s, Ginsburg helped to bring about more equality for both women and men. She also became a role model for young women who were just starting out in their careers. "She was a source of inspiration to all of us," says M. E. Freeman, a New York lawyer who was one of Ginsburg's students in 1976.

But, most important, she helped change the way women were treated in America. As one person pointed out, she almost "single-handedly" forced the Supreme Court to end discrimination against women.

Despite *her heavy work load* during this time, Ginsburg always found time for her family and children. Her second child, James Steven, was born in 1965. James says that his mother always took a special interest in his schoolwork, regardless of how busy she was. "A night did not go by," he says, "when my mother did not check to see that I was doing my schoolwork."

People often asked Ginsburg how she was able to manage a successful and busy career and raise a family at the same time. Her answer was always the same. "If you want to do something badly enough," she said simply, "you find a way. Somehow you manage."

But there was one thing that Ginsburg didn't do at home. That was cook. There was a very simple reason why. Her husband was a much better cook than she. Ginsburg said that her children learned when they were very young that "Daddy was a much better cook than Mommy," and so they forced her out of the kitchen.

When Ginsburg wasn't working or caring for her family, she enjoyed waterskiing, playing golf,

Martin and son, James, take the wheel of a sailboat in this photo of the Ginsburg family at play. Also aboard are Ruth and daughter, Jane, at right.

and riding horses. She also loved opera, old movies, and classical music.

But no matter whether they were at work or leisure, Ginsburg and her husband remained concerned about equal rights. Once in 1980 they invited a black friend to a country club they had just joined. The friend was not treated well by the staff. So the Ginsburgs resigned their membership in the club in protest.

That same year, President Jimmy Carter appointed Ginsburg to the U.S. Court of Appeals for the District of Columbia Circuit, the second highest court in the country. During the next thirteen years, she developed a reputation for being strong but fair as a judge. According to a White House report, she was "tough on crime, committed to free speech and freedom of religion, and supportive of civil rights." This reputation eventually brought Ginsburg to the steps of the Supreme Court.

The Supreme Court of the United States is the highest court in the nation. It has nine members — eight associate justices and one chief justice — all of whom are appointed for life. When a justice dies or retires, the president of the United States nominates someone to fill the vacancy. The U.S. Senate then confirms (approves) or rejects (votes against) the president's choice. Since 1789, when the Supreme Court was established, the Senate has rejected only eleven presidential nominees.

The members of the Supreme Court have one of the most important jobs in the country. Their job is to decide, or rule on, difficult legal questions. Often, they must decide whether federal, state, and local laws are legal. They also must review the rulings of lower courts. To accomplish these tasks, the judges follow the rules and guidelines in the United States Constitution.

The Constitution is what governs our country. It is written, however, in very general terms. Often, people have different opinions about the exact meaning of the Constitution as it applies to modern-day problems or questions. So the members of the Supreme Court must interpret the Constitution. They must decide what the wording of the Constitution really means. And then they must apply the rules to specific cases.

*This sketch shows a case being argued
before the Supreme Court in 1867.*

Each year the Supreme Court receives more than 4,000 requests to hear cases, but only about 150 of those cases are ever argued in front of it. For each request, the nine justices meet to decide whether or not the legal issue in the case is important enough for the Court to rule on it. At least four of the judges must agree to hear the case in order for it to go before the full Supreme Court. If the Court decides not to hear the case, the ruling of the lower court stands.

In ruling on a case, the members of the Supreme Court first listen to arguments for each side of the issue or question. They then meet to discuss the case. Finally, they vote. Cases are decided by majority vote.

The Supreme Court's position on certain issues may change over time. In 1896 the Court said it was legal to have separate facilities for blacks and whites as long as those facilities were equal. That meant there could be one school for whites and a separate school for blacks, as long as both schools provided the same, or equal, education.

But in 1954 the Court changed its mind. It ruled that racially separate schools were not equal. Consequently, the Court ruled that the "separate but equal" law was unconstitutional, meaning it was not legal.

On March 19, 1993, Justice Byron White announced he was going to retire from the Supreme Court at the end of its session, in June. That meant that President Clinton would have to appoint a new justice. It would be the first time a Democratic president appointed a Supreme Court justice in twenty-six years.

President Clinton's staff immediately began to put together a list of possible candidates. Clinton said he wanted someone with a "big heart." Soon more than fifty names were on the list.

Gradually, Clinton narrowed down the list, and by early June reporters said that he had settled on his top three choices — all of whom he believed would be very qualified. One of those choices was Interior Secretary Bruce Babbitt. Another choice was Judge Stephen G. Breyer of the First U.S. Circuit Court of Appeals in Boston. A third choice was Ruth Bader Ginsburg.

Ruth Bader Ginsburg walks with President Clinton outside the White House on Flag Day, the same day he announced her nomination to the Supreme Court.

Clinton had met Ginsburg once only briefly many years earlier. So he invited her to the White House to talk with her. She met the President at 11:00 A.M. on Sunday, June 13, 1993. For the next ninety minutes the two talked about her ideas and opinions on many issues. It was during this conversation that Clinton made up his mind to offer her this all-important job. Later, Clinton told the press, "Once I talked with her, I felt very strongly about her." That night, twelve hours after Clinton had met with Ginsburg, he made the historic phone call to her.

When President Clinton announced his selection for the Supreme Court the next day, almost everyone agreed that Ginsburg was an excellent choice. "Never have I been so . . . pleased with a Supreme Court nominee as I have been with Judge Ginsburg," one senator said. His comment was typical of many.

Even Republicans seemed to like this Democratic president's choice. Bob Dole, the Senate Republican leader, praised Clinton for making a "good choice." He said that Ruth Bader Ginsburg was someone who "undoubtedly has the experience and the intellect to hit the ground running if confirmed."

Ginsburg would become the first Jew to sit on the U.S. Supreme Court in twenty-six years. She would also become only the second woman in history to sit on the Court. (In 1981, President Ronald Reagan appointed Sandra Day O'Connor to the Court.) And the two women justices would sit on the Court at the same time. This was an important fact, according to Ginsburg. She explained her feelings in this way. "The announcement the President just made is significant, I believe, because it contributes to the end of the day when women, at least half the talent pool in our society, appear in high places only as one-at-a-time performers."

In July 1993 the United States Senate met with Judge Ginsburg. They asked her about her views on many topics, as millions of Americans watched the hearings on television. Ginsburg impressed almost everyone with her even-tempered, thoughtful answers to the senators' questions. Then the Senate voted on whether or not to confirm her

Ginsburg holds up a message from her grandson during the hearings at which senators questioned her about her views.

Here, nominee Ginsburg takes questions from schoolchildren. Senator Joseph Biden is standing next to her.

nomination to the Supreme Court. Senator Daniel Patrick Moynihan of New York had predicted that she would be confirmed by a vote of 100 to 0. He was almost right. The final vote was 96 in favor of confirmation and only 3 against. (One senator did not vote.)

On August 10, 1993, Supreme Court Justice William Rehnquist swore in Ruth Bader Ginsburg to the Supreme Court. It was a momentous occasion. As Justice Ginsburg thought about the responsibilities that lay ahead, she must have also thought back twenty years to 1973. That year, her daughter graduated from high school. The editors of the student yearbook listed the ambition of each senior next to his or her picture. Next to Jane's picture, it said that her ambition was to see her mother sit on the U.S. Supreme Court. Then it added: "If necessary, Jane will appoint her." Thanks to President Clinton, she didn't have to.

As Ginsburg took her seat on the High Court, many people wondered: What kind of Supreme Court justice would she be? Perhaps the answer could be found in her own words about judges in general. "The greatest figures of the American ju-

From a podium, Chief Justice William Rehnquist swears in Ruth Bader Ginsburg. At her left is her husband; President Clinton stands behind her.

Ruth Bader Ginsburg, the 107th justice of the United States Supreme Court, takes her place among the other justices in this photo.

diciary," she said, "have been independent thinking individuals with open but not empty minds — individuals willing to listen and to learn." Most people who know her would agree that Ruth Bader Ginsburg, the 107th justice of the United States Supreme Court, is that kind of person.

Important Dates

March 15, 1933   Ruth Joan Bader is born in Brooklyn, New York.

June 1954   Graduates from Cornell University in Ithaca, New York.

June 23, 1954   Marries Martin David Ginsburg.

1959   Graduates from Columbia University Law School; ties for first in her class.

1963   Becomes assistant professor of law at Rutgers University in New Jersey.

1972   Becomes the first woman to be hired by Columbia University as a full-tenured professor.

1970s   Argues six important sex discrimination cases in front of the U.S. Supreme Court; wins five.

1980   Appointed to the U.S. Court of Appeals for the District of Columbia Circuit by President Jimmy Carter.

June 14, 1993   Nominated to the U.S. Supreme Court by President Bill Clinton.

August 10, 1993   Sworn in as the 107th justice of the Supreme Court, and becomes only the second woman to serve on the Court.

Find Out More

About the United States Supreme Court

Sandra Day O'Connor by Beverley Gherman. New York: Viking, 1991.

The Story of the Powers of the Supreme Court by Conrad R. Stein. Chicago: Childrens Press, 1989.

The Supreme Court by Rae Bains. Mahwah, N.J.: Troll Associates, 1985.

The Supreme Court by Carol Greene. Chicago: Childrens Press, 1985.

About Discrimination

Discrimination by Gail Stewart. New York: Crestwood House, 1989.

About Women's Careers

Women at Their Work by Betty L. English. New York: Dial Books, 1989.

Index